GUARD YOUR
PEACE

A SCREENPLAY BY FELICIA GUY-LYNCH

ISBN-13: 978-0987969361

Dedication
To all those cultivating peace

GUARD YOUR PEACE

Preface

This book is the fourth short story to The *Finding Isaiah* series. It's the final draft of the screenplay before production.

Check out the short film on the Si Obi Nation YouTube or Vimeo page!

Sincerely,

Felicia Guy-Lynch

1 INT. SPA - DAY

Upscale and warm with an elegant layout. A spa fit for a king. ISAIAH JOHNSON, 25, walks into the soothing spa and approaches the empty reception desk. He RINGS the counter bell for service. A CLIENT steps out from one of the rooms followed by RENEE GRANT, 24. ISAIAH glances quickly at RENEE. RENEE glances back while still speaking to her CLIENT. Never forgetting that face, she relieves her CLIENT with a smile and starts to approach ISAIAH. ISAIAH tries to not notice her. RENEE stands behind the reception desk.

                    RENEE
    What a pleasant surprise! How may I help you?

                    ISAIAH
         Renee. I didn't know you work here.

                    RENEE
      Yep. I've owned this place for a month now.

                    ISAIAH
    Isn't that a coincidence? My shop is just a few blocks
                     west.

                    RENEE
   Mmm. Still ambitious I see. I guess it's meant to be.

                    ISAIAH
              What do you mean?

RENEE walks around the desk to get closer to ISAIAH.

RENEE
Us. Crossing paths. Having our own businesses just
down the street from each other.

She starts stroking his chest while moving in closer.

RENEE (CONT'D)
Listen hun: whenever you're in need to relieve some ten-
sion, you know where to find me.

She bites her lips with a smirk. ISAIAH kindly removes
her hadn't.

ISAIAH
Renee, look...

RENEE walks back around the desk and starts going
through papers, picks a clipboard.

RENEE
Oh, come on. Lighten up, Isaiah. We both know we have
some catching up to do. So, let's not put up a front now.

He smiles, shakes his head and walks toward the door.

RENEE (CONT'D)
I see you still have no manners.

ISAIAH waves from behind and exits the spa. RENEE
shakes her head and smiles while focusing back on work
as another CLIENT approaches the desk.

2 INT. BEDROOM - NIGHT

The bedroom is well kept. NAOMI JOHNSON, 25, enters the bedroom to give ISAIAH a glass of water and Advil. ISAIAH is lying down on the bed.

> ISAIAH
> Thanks, babe. You're the best.

NAOMI leans over to kiss ISAIAH on the forehead.

> NAOMI
> I know.

ISAIAH takes the pills and washes them down with the water.

NAOMI caresses ISAIAH'S head.

> ISAIAH
> Dinner was delicious by the way.

> NAOMI
> Glad you enjoyed.

ISAIAH finishes the water and puts the glass down on the nightstand.

> ISAIAH
> Oh. Guess who I ran into today?

> NAOMI
> Jeonsa?

> ISAIAH
> Nope.

> NAOMI
> Then who?

> ISAIAH
> (hesitates)
> Renee.

NAOMI rolls her eyes. Sighs and then gets up to go change into nightclothes.

> ISAIAH (CONT'D)
> She opened up her own spa close by the shop.

NAOMI comes back to her side of the bed.

> NAOMI
> (kisses her teeth)
> The bitch can go kick rocks.

NAOMI makes herself comfortable in bed.

> ISAIAH
> I'm on board with you but unfortunately, she's the only one with the answers I need.

ISAIAH turns around to face NAOMI, climbs on top of her and caresses her face.

> NAOMI
> I just want to pick up where we left off. I'm finally at peace with the past behind us.

ISAIAH kisses NAOMI'S neck.

> ISAIAH
> I know.

NAOMI looks up.

> ISAIAH (CONT'D)
> You ok?

> NAOMI
> Yea. I'm fine.

ISAIAH stares into NAOMI'S eyes, leans in and starts kissing her.

> NAOMI (CONT'D)
> We can't make love tonight. It's that time again. Remember?

> ISAIAH
> That's alright. We have other ways around that.

ISAIAH kisses her again.

> NAOMI
> Not tonight baby. I just want to relax in your arms. Okay? It's been a long day and these cramps are finally starting to let up.

ISAIAH
(sighs)
Alright. Alright. I got you.

ISAIAH turns on his side, holding NAOMI from the back.

NAOMI closes her eyes and then opens them again slow-ly.

3 INT. BEDROOM - MORNING

ISAIAH pauses when he sees his IPHONE FLASH WITH A TEXT.

ISAIAH picks up the phone and dials RENEE'S number. As we pull back, he stops himself and hangs up the phone.

ISAIAH stares at the time.

ISAIAH redials her number. THREE RINGS and then it goes to voicemail.

RENEE
Hey. You've reached Renee Grant. Please leave your name and number and I'll get back to you as soon as possible.

RENEE is calling on the other line. ISAIAH ends the voicemail to answer her call.

ISAIAH
Hello?

RENEE
Hey you! What's up?

ISAIAH
Nothing much. I was actually thinking of booking an appointment at your spa.

INTERCUT SCENES BETWEEN PHONE CONVERSA-
TION:

4 INT. SPA - MORNING

The spa is quite busy. Different clients sitting patiently and others chatting with some employees. Calm MUSIC fills the air. RENEE is walking around while cradling the phone.

RENEE
Where are you, hun?

ISAIAH
Home.

RENEE
So. When would you like to book an appointment?

ISAIAH
Whenever you're available.

RENEE acknowledges a client.

RENEE
I'll be right with you. Well, okay. I can schedule you in for 2pm today.

ISAIAH
That works. I'll be there a quarter to.

ISAIAH stares at NAOMI'S picture for a while.

GUARD YOUR PEACE

5 INT. SPA - AFTERNOON

The spa has less traffic as ISAIAH enters. RENEE is standing by the receptionist's desk, waiting with a welcoming grin.

ISAIAH walks to the desk and approaches RENEE and LISA WILSON, 22.

> RENEE
> Ready to relieve some tension, Mr. Johnson?

> ISAIAH
> It depends.

> RENEE
> Well. Your room is second to the left when you finish pending.

ISAIAH smiles and walks down the hall, scoping out the place and checks out a next masseuse.

RENEE and LISA are still watching him.

> RENEE
> Lisa. Do you mind closing tonight?

LISA smiles as RENEE picks up the fresh towels.

> LISA
> That's what's up. Of course, I will, Ms. Hot Foot.

RENEE
Shut up.

RENEE smiles as she hits LISA with the towel jokingly.

6 INT. SPA - AFTERNOON

The room is lit with candles and decorated with fresh flowers. The tone is intimate. ISAIAH looks around the room and takes off his coat and places it on the chair. RENEE enters the room with the towels.

RENEE
(licking her lips)
Please believe you are in the right place at the right time.

ISAIAH
Actually. I came to get an Ionic Foot Bath.

RENEE
Really? Oh…okay. I'll plug in the machine and get fresh towels. Put your feet in the machine after you take off your shoes and socks.

30 minutes later, RENEE enters the room again.

RENEE
How's everything going?

ISAIAH
Everything is everything.

RENEE
You know you're my last client. Want to go grab a nite after?

ISAIAH
Are you treating me?

                    RENEE
                    Depends.

ISAIAH places his hand on his chin.

                    ISAIAH
                    Yea. Why not?

ISAIAH and RENEE both smile at each other.

7 INT. COFFEE SHOP - EARLY AFTERNOON

A comfortable home-style setup. CUSTOMERS relaxing, on laptops and having a conversation. RENEE and ISA-IAH are enjoying each other's company. ISAIAH puts his keys and phone on the table. Food and drinks are being enjoyed.

RENEE
(while laughing)
You crack me up. So stupid.

RENEE hits ISAIAH.

ISAIAH
I try.

ISAIAH and RENEE smile and then ISAIAH'S IPHONE RINGS. He motions RENEE to be quiet as he grins and then answers the phone. RENEE picks up her drink.

ISAIAH

Hey Love...Yeah. My day was great... Yeah... That's great... Okay hun. Save the details for me when I get home. Yeah...I'm just in a meeting... Okay? Alright... I love you too.

RENEE sips her drink.

RENEE
Wifey?

ISAIAH
Yeah.

RENEE
So. How is Naomi?

ISAIAH
She's nice. Still doing her thing. But I really want to talk
about something else. It has been on my mind for five
long years.

RENEE
(hesitantly)
So. That's what this is about? Haze? The man is dead.
What more do you want?

ISAIAH
I just want to know if you had anything to do with Naomi's
kidnapping. Was it something you told Haze?

RENEE stares at ISAIAH in disbelief.

RENEE
I don't have time for this.

RENEE gathers her belongings and proceeds to exit.
ISAIAH reaches out her arm. RENEE looks at ISAIAH.

ISAIAH
Please. I just want closure.

RENEE bows and nods her head down. Sighs and proceeds to sit back down.

ISAIAH
Thank you.

A WAITER interrupts.

WAITER
Is everything alright here? Would you like some tea? Coffee?

ISAIAH
We're fine. Thanks.

The WAITER walks away to tend to other CUSTOMERS. ISAIAH focuses back on RENEE. RENEE is caught up in her thoughts.

ISAIAH (CONT'D)
Renee...

RENEE
(starts to tear up)
Haze was sick in his head. He was very emotionally and physically abusive. He used to insist something was going on between us but I kept reassuring him that we weren't doing anything. I was faithful to him. But Haze was always one way with you but another way with me. In my opinion, I think he was jealous of you. That's why he went as far as to kidnap Naomi. I had nothing to do with his madness.

ISAIAH reaches out to touch her hand.
ISAIAH

This whole time I was upset with you because I thought you were behind the kidnapping. I just needed closure. That's all. You understand?

                    RENEE
I do. Glad you feel differently now.

                    ISAIAH
Well. Yeah. After you telling me this, it explains why he went coo coo. That's why I had to take him out.

RENEE wipes her tears.

                    RENEE
It was one of the best things you could have done. You freed me. Allowed me to pursue my dreams. I've always loved you, Isaiah.

RENEE rests her hand on ISAIAH'S hand and looks him deep in his eyes.

                    RENEE (CONT'D)
Always will. Let me take care of you.

ISAIAH removes his hand, hesitantly.

                    ISAIAH
                    (beat)
Renee. We can't do this. Why are you still pursuing me?

                    RENEE

Because you have a certain peace about you I always
wanted to be a part of.

ISAIAH
What do you mean?

RENEE gazes into ISAIAH'S eyes.

RENEE
Just the way you are. I feel protected by your presence
and you're not even my man.

ISAIAH looks away.

ISAIAH
Wow.

RENEE
Men like you are so rare. Especially in these times.

ISAIAH
I'm speechless.

RENEE grabs his hand once more. RENEE and ISAIAH
gaze into each other's eyes.

ISAIAH
(hesitantly)
Renee. I shouldn't be doing this with you.

RENEE leans in slowly towards ISAIAH.

RENEE
If that's the case, why haven't you left yet?

ISAIAH can't face her. ISAIAH heads for the door.

ISAIAH
I gotta go.

Not looking back, ISAIAH exits the coffee shop. RENEE spots ISAIAH's car keys on the table.

RACK FOCUS BETWEEN KEYS AND RENEE:

RENEE picks up the keys, gathers her belongings, leaves the coffee shop to catch up with ISAIAH.

8 EXT. PARKING LOT - MORNING

ISAIAH paces to his vehicle as he checks his pockets for his keys. He stops while searching his pockets.

> ISAIAH
> Shit. Don't tell me I forgot my keys.

RENEE reaches out to give him his keys. They look each other in the eyes once more. And just like that, he pulls her in for a passionate kiss.

9 INT. ISAIAH'S CAR - NIGHT

ISAIAH pulls up on the highway, turns his emergency lights on, staring out the driver's window as the cars pass him by.

ISAIAH bows his head and is staring at his wedding ban.

10 INT. RENEE'S BEDROOM - NIGHT

Three flashbacks of the lovemaking between ISAIAH and RENEE.

11 INT. BEDROOM - NIGHT

ISAIAH is lying down in the bed with Felicia Guy-Lynch's *365* in his hand but isn't really reading the book. NAOMI enters from the bathroom with one towel around her body and one around her head.

She stares at him as she starts to dry her hair.

> NAOMI
> Everything okay?

> ISAIAH
> Yea...

> NAOMI
> Okay?...

ISAIAH starts to read, paying NAOMI no mind.

> NAOMI (CONT'D)
> How about lunch after my workout tomorrow?

> ISAIAH
> Oh yeah?

> NAOMI
> Did I catch you off guard?

> ISAIAH
> Actually, I have a Muay Thai session with Jeonsa. I have some catching up to do.

NAOMI
Then we can meet after your session.

ISAIAH
Babe. I would love that but it's been a while. I might stay
longer than usual. You understand. Right?

NAOMI
Yea. You gotta do what you gotta do.

ISAIAH smiles and NAOMI puts her hands on his face
and leans him in for a kiss.

NAOMI
Tell Jeonsa I said he owes me one.

ISAIAH
Will do.

NAOMI
Good night.

ISAIAH
Good night.

NAOMI kisses ISAIAH good night. He tucks himself into
bed. She is still up.

12 INT. KITCHEN - EVENING

NAOMI is preparing dinner in the kitchen as ISAIAH walks in and starts to stare at NAOMI. She pays no attention to him.

ISAIAH
Sorry, I'm late. Traffic was hectic on the road...

NAOMI
That's fine.

ISAIAH
What did you make for dinner?

NAOMI
I'm going to Brampton tomorrow.

ISAIAH
Why?

NAOMI
To meet with Mom.

ISAIAH
When are you coming back?

NAOMI
Tomorrow night.

ISAIAH
So what time are you leaving?

NAOMI
Seven. Come with me.

ISAIAH
I'll take a breather. It's been a hectic couple of days.

NAOMI
It's been so long since we've seen your Mom. She would
love to see you as well.

ISAIAH
That's true but we're going to see her next week for her
birthday. It can wait.

ISAIAH (CONT'D)
What?

NAOMI
You tell me.

13 INT. BEDROOM - EARLY MORNING

ISAIAH is asleep. NAOMI leans down to kiss ISAIAH. NAOMI looks at ISAIAH for a couple of seconds. NAOMI leaves. ISAIAH'S eyes open.

14 INT. BEDROOM - MORNING

ISAIAH turns off the tap after washing his face and stares in the mirror.

15 INT. NAOMI'S HOTEL SUITE - DAY

NAOMI is making passionate love to JEONSA. She is performing the cowgirl while JEONSA has both his hands on her breasts. JEONSA exits the hotel and heads to-wards his vehicle.

16 EXT. HIGHWAY - AFTERNOON

CLOSE UP on JEONSA driving on the highway. He's on his way to teach students at his training studio. CLOSE UP on RENEE driving on the highway. She's on her way to go see ISAIAH at his house. CLOSE UP on RENEE texting ISAIAH. BLACK SCREEN with car crash sound effects. Two cars are met in a bad collision.

17 INT. NAOMI'S HOTEL SUITE - AFTERNOON

NAOMI uses the remote to turn on the television and watches the 6 o'clock news with heightened interest. She recognizes JEONSA'S car.

18 INT. ISAIAH'S BEDROOM - AFTERNOON

ISAIAH uses the remote to turn on the television and watches the 6 o'clock news with heightened interest. He recognizes RENNE'S car.

19 EXT. CAR ACCIDENT - AFTERNOON

ISAIAH and NAOMI go to the sight of the car accident at the same time. NAOMI sees ISAIAH.

20 INT. LIVING ROOM - AFTERNOON

The place is dark, NAOMI turns on the light and puts down her keys. ISAIAH follows suit. NAOMI starts to clean up the living room.

ISAIAH
What are the odds of us reaching home at the same time?

ISAIAH cracks a smile but NAOMI remains serious.

NAOMI
I'm not sure but the odds are against us.

ISAIAH
Is it? Since when did you start wearing shirts inside out?

NAOMI stops to realize her shirt.

NAOMI
I had to rush.

NAOMI continues cleaning.

ISAIAH
Are you okay?

NAOMI stops and starts to stare at ISAIAH.

NAOMI
Do you love me, Isaiah?

ISAIAH
Does that wedding band say otherwise?

NAOMI
When your feelings changed, did you care to keep me in
the loop?

ISAIAH looks at NAOMI puzzled, avoids the question.
ISAIAH moves towards her.

ISAIAH
What? What are you -

NAOMI
How about you come clean?

ISAIAH is surprised at NAOMI's strong demand.

NAOMI (CONT'D)
How could you be so careless?

ISAIAH
Baby...

NAOMI

Don't baby me. Keep that to yourself. I gave you everything. But no, all of me isn't good enough. Eh? What's it
called again? Oh yeah: the 80/20 rule you men go by.
The thing is I'm not just 80% of anything. I'm 100% in all
that I've offered you. But what do you go do? Sleep with
Renee. "Unanswered questions" my ass.

ISAIAH sighs.

NAOMI (CONT'D)

That's why I screwed Jeonsa!

ISAIAH stares at NAOMI.

NAOMI

I didn't want to screw him. I wanted to make love to you
but you pushed me away.

ISAIAH is absolutely stunned at what NAOMI told him.

ISAIAH

Of all people. Jeonsa?

NAOMI does not respond.

ISAIAH (CONT'D)

Wow. That's fucked up.

ISAIAH is shocked. She heads to the bathroom. We stay
on ISAIAH'S face as we hear NAOMI go upstairs. He
puts his hands on his face.

GUARD YOUR PEACE

21 INT. BEDROOM - NIGHT

NAOMI is lying down on her side of the bed. ISAIAH enters the bedroom and sits on the edge of the bed.

NAOMI
How did we come to this?

ISAIAH
I don't know but I want to make it up to you.

NAOMI
Did you love her?

ISAIAH
I bumped into her. And out of nowhere, things I've never imagine possible started flooding my mind.

NAOMI
I can say the same thing about myself.

ISAIAH
I didn't love her. You'll always be my Queen.

CU on NAOMI crying. He comforts her from behind. We PULL back to a wide shot on the two cuddling.

FADE OUT:
END CREDITS

www.ingramcontent.com/pod-product-compliance
Lightning Source LLC
Chambersburg PA
CBHW070117070426
42448CB00040B/3123